SCOTTISH SUP GUIDE

Where to Stand Up Paddleboard in Scotland

Matt Gambles

Paddle Surf Scotland

CONTENTS

Title Page	
SUP in Scotland	1
Region by Region	2
When to Go	5
How to get around	6
Edinburgh and the Lothians	7
Belhaven Beach	8
Fidra Island and Yellowcraig Beach	10
The Borders and the South West	12
Coldingham Bay	13
Glasgow and Ayrshire	14
Loch Lomond	15
Fife and Angus	17
Lunan Bay	18
Elie and the East Neuk	20
St Andrews	22
Perthshire and the Central Highlands	24
Loch Lubhair and Loch Dochart	25
Loch Earn	27
Loch Lubnaig	29
Loch Venacher	30

Loch Tay West, Killin	31
Loch Tay East, Kenmore	33
Loch Rannoch	36
Loch Tummel	38
Clunie Loch	40
River Isla, Coupar Angus	42
Adventurous Perthshire Lochs - Bike or Hike to a Hidden Gem	44
River Tummel - Pitlochry to Ballinluig	46
River Tay, Dunkeld, Perthshire	48
River Tay - Dunkeld to Caputh	51
River Tay - Stanley to Thistlebrig - Whitewater	53
Loch Freuchie and the River Quaich, Perthshire	56
Aberdeen and the North East	59
Nairn	60
Hopeman	62
Lossiemouth	64
Argyll and the Great Glen	66
Arisaig	67
Sanna Bay	69
Glencoe, Loch Leven	71
Kerrera	73
Castle Stalker	75
Loch Ness	77
Loch Morlich	79
The Northern Highlands and the North Coast 500	81
The North Coast 500 - A Paddleboard Guide to the Ultimate Road Trip	82
Gairloch	86

Badachro	88
Poolewe	89
Achmelvich	91
Dunnet Beach	93
Strathy	95
Durness	97
About The Author	99

SUP IN SCOTLAND

From the pumping surf of the North Shore, the white sands of the west coast, the open lochs of the Highlands or the living history along it's Rivers, Scotland has it all. With buzzing cities, unique food, great live music and welcoming locals, it surely has to be one of the best and varied Paddleboarding locations in the World.

In this Guide, we hope to be able to show you a little taste of what Scotland has to offer. But with thousands of miles of Coastline, hundreds of Lochs and numerous Rivers we are merely scratching the surface of where you can go. With the Scottish Access Code giving you a huge amount of access rights to where you can go, it could be a never ending journey of discovery in what Scotland has to Paddleboard.

We have included a vast array of different locations in the Guide, hopefully it will have something for everyone, from the most hardcore of Surfer to those wanting a gentle, scenic paddle.

REGION BY REGION

Edinburgh and the Lothians - Scotland's Capital City is a must see destination. With it's Castle dominating the skyline, it's Old Town and 18th Century New Town, there is plenty to see and history to immerse yourself in. With plenty of pubs, clubs and World Class eateries, plus the Edinburgh Festival the most celebrated arts Festival on the Planet, there is always something going on.

In and around Edinburgh there are some superb paddling opportunities, from admiring the views of the Firth of Forth to the surf breaks south of the City in the Lothians.

The Borders and the South West - The numerous Abbeys of the Scottish Borders are set within idyllic rolling hills, perfect for getting away from it all. Flowing past many of these Abbeys is the River Tweed, offering some great sections to Paddleboard. On its shoreline, several of the East Coast's best surf breaks can be found.

The South West of Scotland, the county of Dumfries and Galloway is full of wide open spaces, huge forests and incredible scenery to be enjoyed from the water.

Glasgow and Ayrshire - Glasgow is the Country's largest City and it's pulsing, throbbing heart. Expect lively nights, great shopping and World Class Art Galleries. Just North of the City is the famous Bonny Banks of Loch Lomond, one of Scotland's biggest and most majestic pieces of water.

South of the City is the Ayrshire countryside, made famous by the poems of Robert Burns. With a variety of great places to paddle, especially the large Island of Arran, there are incredible views to enjoy from the water.

Fife and Angus - With sandy beaches and quaint fishing villages, the eastern tip of the 'Kingdom' of Fife's coastline has plenty to enjoy. It's nooks and crannies are ideal to explore from your Paddleboard. The town of St Andrews is World famous for its Golf courses and university, this must see town also has lovely beaches, surf and a great paddle underneath it's cliffs.

North of Fife and the up and coming City of Dundee lies the County of Angus. It has some fantastic beaches to enjoy, especially Lunan Bay.

Perthshire and the Central Highlands - This is where for many the traditional idea of Scotland will come to life. Mountains and glens with water cascading down them into its many Lochs. With plenty of small welcoming towns and villages as well as the two Cities of Stirling and Perth, there is a huge amount to explore.

There are Lochs of different sizes to explore in addition to several of Scotland's most paddleable Rivers, notably the Forth, Earn and the Tay.

Aberdeen and the North East - The Granite City of Aberdeen has some fantastic beaches and surf in and around it. The Rivers Dee and Don both flow into the City, both of which have plenty of touring potential.

The North East and Moray coasts are packed with little fishing villages offering excellent paddling in coves, under cliffs and by it's beaches. This is a great surf location, with Fraserburgh, Banff and Sandend being particularly blessed!. The Moray Firth is an excellent spot to see Dolphins.

Argyll and the Great Glen - From the high slopes of Ben Nevis to the big waves at the Mull of Kintyre, this area is hewn from the elemental forces of nature. With long forks of Lochs stretching inland from the sea underneath Britain's biggest Mountains, the views from your board can be breathtaking.

The White sand beaches and turquoise waters of Arisaig and Sanna Bay are a fantastic compliment to the Paddleboarding on the inspiring Lochs.

The Highlands and North Coast 500 - The mighty Scottish Highlands, it evokes empty spaces, brooding mountains, fantastic wildlife, dark lochs and churning seas. All of these are true but with plenty of surprising sights along the way.....from tropical plants growing on the water's edge, white sand beaches and World Class Surf breaks.

The North Coast 500 route takes in much of the best of what the Highlands has to offer. For the adventurous Stand Up Paddleboarder this could be the ultimate bucket list trip.

The Scottish Isles - Orkney, Shetland, Skye, Outer Hebrides... places that attract the adventurous, the romantic, the inquisitive. Time on the Scottish Islands rewards those with patience, happy to take whatever the weather throws at them. With incredible surf, white sandy beaches and tiny lochans hidden away, you are likely to have your bit of paddling paradise to yourself.

In this Book we concentrate on Paddle Boarding destinations on or from the Scottish Mainland, the Islands of Scotland offer a whole other World of Paddle opportunities.

WHEN TO GO

Spring - Scotland comes out of hibernation and the days become longer. Expect all types of weather in a single day. Indeed it is very much possible to both Ski and Paddleboard in the same day.

Summer - With long hours of daylight (in the far North it can feel like the sun never sets), the water and air temperatures increase, bringing some balmy wonderful days to paddle. Scotland comes alive in the Summer with festivals galore and lots going on.

Autumn - The days shorten, yet the water temperatures stay remarkably resilient. The Surf starts to come alive and it is an excellent time to find swell. The changing of the colour of the leaves on the trees surrounding the Lochs and Rivers create an incredible visual feast.

Winter - The days shorten as the surf size increases. There are still plenty of Paddleboarders and Surfers heading out in the Winter, enjoying the plentiful swell and higher river levels. It can be extremely cold at times during a Scottish Winter so make sure you are prepared and have plenty of warm gear.

HOW TO GET AROUND

Scotland has International airports at Edinburgh, Glasgow, Glasgow Prestwick, Inverness and Aberdeen. There are plenty of connections from London and other UK airports. Logan Air offers flights to many of the Scottish Islands.

The National Rail network is quick and efficient with Edinburgh and Glasgow as the national hubs. A sleeper service connects the far North of the country with London.

The long haul buses in Scotland are usually run by Citylink with cheap intercity connections on its subsidiary, Megabus. Onwards travel to the rest of the UK is by Megabus or National Express.

To travel to the Islands, the Ferries are run by Caledonian Macbrayne. For travel to the Orkneys and Shetland, Northlink is the main Ferry provider, along with some others on the shorter Caithness to Orkney route. It is important to book well ahead of you want to take a car onboard.

There are plentiful Car hire companies throughout Scotland and the Isles. Cars drive on the left and you will require a full international driving license.

EDINBURGH AND THE LOTHIANS

BELHAVEN BEACH

Just outside the town of Dunbar and backed by the trees and dunes of the John Muir Country Park lies Belhaven Bay. This large stretch of golden sands means there is plenty of space to a leisurely paddle or the start of a commiting journey under the cliffs of the town to Dunbar Harbour. Belhaven is also the nearest place to Edinburgh to pick up some consistent surf. There is a friendly crew here and the size of the places means that there are usually plenty of waves to share around. From the most powerful waves in the centre of the bay to longer mellow peaks nearer to the car park entry point listed in the co-ordinates, there are plenty of Paddleboarding friendly waves to be had here.

From the car park, looking across towards the beach you will see the unique 'Bridge to Nowhere', a tiny walking bridge for beach goers at lower tides, at High tide it is surrounded by the sea. This makes it a great photo opportunity while also being aware you might get wet
getting back to your car at High tide or take a long long walk around it.

Co-ordinates
55.999961,-2.543568

Nearest Place
Dunbar contains plenty of shops and restaurants, plus places to stay.

Off the Water
Foxlake Cable Wakeboarding.
Just outside Dunbar and in a lovely Wooded setting is the Foxlake

Wakeboarding Loch. With a system 2.0 cable, jumps and rails, it's a great place to ride, whether beginner or expert.
https://www.foxlake.co.uk/

FIDRA ISLAND AND YELLOWCRAIG BEACH

Situated on the East Lothian Coast and south of Edinburgh lies Yellowcraig beach. It's a gently sloping coved beach with rockpools and small escarpments jutting out into the sea. This lovely setting is a fantastic place to go Paddle Boarding with views North to the Fife Coast and south to the Imposing Volcanic Bass Rock to the South. The view inland is of small dunes and Forest.

What makes Yellowcraig stand out even more is the Island of Fidra which sits about 300m off its shore. Paddling to Fidra is committing and needs to be undertaken with ideal conditions and the requisite experience.

Fidra is the inspiration for the Scottish writer Robert Louis Stevenson's most famous novel, Treasure Island. It also houses a picture perfect Lighthouse, dating from 1885.

Paddling around Fidra to its seaward side offers fantastic Birdwatching. Indeed, the name Fidra comes from an old Norse word, meaning 'feather island'. Puffins are regularly seen on the cliffs. The Island is owned by the Royal Society for the Protection of Birds (RSPB) so please be respectful to the area and its wildlife while paddling nearby and do not land on the Island.

Co-ordinates
56.060509,-2.778868
Please be aware of the height barriers to the car park if you have boards on your roof.

Nearest Place
There are toilets at the car park with the nearby village of Direlton having shops, eateries and more.

Off the Water
Dirleton Castle. With its impressive gardens and Towers dating back to 1250, there is plenty to admire and immerse yourself in.
https://www.historicenvironment.scot/visit-a-place/places/dirleton-castle/

THE BORDERS AND THE SOUTH WEST

COLDINGHAM BAY

Down South, near the English Border lies the fantastic surf spot of Coldingham Bay. Backed by cliffs (and with plenty of spectacular coastal walks leading off from it), Coldingham is a protected One Kilometre wide cove of rock and sand. It has several peaks depending on the tide, and is usually pretty quiet.

The cliffs and the steep hill leading down to the beach offer a significant amount of protection from the prevailing offshore winds which the East Coast has. This also means that on flat days this may be the least windy spot on this coast for a calm flat water paddle in relative safety.

Co-ordinates
Eyemouth TD14 5PA

Nearest Place
At the beach is St Vedas Hotel, with accommodation, food, toilets and a Surf Shop.
The beach is just outside the lovely conservation village of Coldingham. It has a shop plus a few places to eat and stay. For more options, the Fishing port of Eyemouth is just 3 miles South.

Off the Water
St Abbs Nature Reserve. The huge cliffs just North at St Abbs are a fantastic place to admire the thousands of Birds that call it home. Puffins can be spotted along with Guillemots, Razorbills and Kittiwakes.
https://www.nts.org.uk/visit/places/st-abbs-head

GLASGOW AND AYRSHIRE

LOCH LOMOND

The Bonnie, Bonnie Banks of Loch Lomond are celebrated in Song and the deep mythology of Scotland. The Biggest Loch, by area, in Scotland is also its most visited. Sitting just outside Glasgow, it has been the lungs and place to escape to for the city for centuries. It is easy to see why, it's a magnificent place with so many places to see, secret corners to explore and islands to tick off. All the while the hills loom down on it, especially Ben Lomond, creating magnificent reflections.

It is a huge expanse of water with plenty of places to see and get in. The weather makes a huge difference and it can be a serious place to be out on the water, so , as always be prepared, experienced and knowledgeable on conditions before going out.

The very far north of the Loch at Ardlui tends to be slightly more sheltered overall than most parts. It's where the Loch becomes less wide and the hills give plenty of protection.

Further south, the main road artery, the A82 offers many waterside locations to launch from, we particularly enjoy getting on in busy Luss and exploring some of the smaller islands just offshore, a great juxtaposition of quiet and buzzing places.

At the southernmost point of Loch Lomond is Balloch. It's a busy little place, boats coming and going, lively marinas and certainly not the Loch destination for peace and quiet. But it's an excellent place to Paddle and soak up the energy of one of Glasgow's most popular bolt holes.

On its slightly quieter Western shore, the little B837 winds along its shoreline. Balmaha and Milarrochy Bay are excellent places to launch from and visit the Lomond Islands. Our favourite is right at the very end of the road, where the Ben Lomond walkers car park is right on the Loch with stunning views to admire from the water. The winds tend to be more onshore on the eastern Loch so it's again something to be aware.

Co-ordinates
Ardlui - 56.303734,-4.720585
Luss - 56.102819,-4.638918
Balloch - 56.007911,-4.589768
Ben Lomond Car Park - Ben Lomond Car Park, Stirling, Glasgow G63 0AR

Nearest Place
Situated North of Glasgow, you will find plenty of facilities, places to stay and eat in the touristy settlements along the banks. Balloch in particular has everything you will need. There is no Wild Camping in the entire Loch Lomond and the Trossachs National Park but there are several commercial campsites.

Off the Water
Loch Lomond Wakeboarding. Situated at Ardlui and enjoying the calm conditions this part of the Loch can have is this excellent centre. Learn to Wakeboard, Water Ski and Wake Surf.
https://www.lochlomondwakeboard.com/

FIFE AND ANGUS

LUNAN BAY

Probably the jewel in the crown of the East Coast's beaches, this huge horseshoe bay is halfway between Arbroath and Montrose on the Angus Coast. With a central car park, just a wander over the views from the water, a cafe and campsite, it's a great destination. The view from the top of the dunes is spectacular with cliffs rising at both ends of the beach.

In perfect conditions, a paddle to the north from the main beach and up to the ruined Boddin Lime Kilns makes a great day out. Paddling through rock pools, under cliffs and through kelp beds, all in spectacular coastal scenery, this is a fantastic, through committing paddle.

Lunan Bay is one of the East Coast's top surfing destinations, with plenty of powerful peaks along its length. It's best on the pushing tide from Mid to High, as it doesn't tend to work at Low tide.

Watch out for strong rips when there is surf here, especially around the entrance to Lunan Burn where it drains into the sea. Also be aware that the prevailing wind is offshore on Scotland's East Coast.

Co-ordinates
56.655274,-2.505503

Nearest Place
Halfway between the two towns of Montrose and Arbroath. Both have plenty of facilities and are well worth an explore, especially Arbroath's Abbey and it's Marina area.

Off the Water

Arbroath is famous for its local delicacy, the Smokie. A lightly smoked whole haddock, it is delicious and can be purchased directly from the smokehouses in and around the harbour.

ELIE AND THE EAST NEUK

The East Neuk of Fife, on the Peninsula's southern coast is a string of magnificent, quaint Fishing villages. They are all fantastic destinations in their own rights, each one with their own flavours. Several have secluded little Harbours which are still active, so expect to see small trawlers and photogenic Lobster Pots scattered around. In and around these small harbours you will find cliffs and some fairly secluded beaches to explore.

Facing South as this coastline does, the wind tends to blow cross-shore so be aware of the wind direction (and your skill levels) as well as the tide, when choosing where, if or when to get in.

Elie at the Western end of the East Neuk is a lovely family seaside resort with a wide sandy bay, making it a slightly more sheltered location than the more exposed East Neuk coastline elsewhere. It is a fairly shallow bay and a lovely place to spend an afternoon Paddleboarding. Looking across the Sea and the Firth of Forth to the South of Elie, admire the views of East Lothian, Bass Rock and on a good day, the Northumberland coastline.

Co-ordinates
Elie - Elie, Leven KY9 1EG

Nearest Place
Elie and the East Neil villages (the main ones being Crail, Anstruther and Pitenweem) all have a good array of shops, eateries and places to stay.

Off the Water
The Secret Bunker. 100ft underground is a huge array of tunnels and equipment for what would have been the Scottish Government's base in case of Nuclear War. A fascinating and unique attraction.
www.secretbunker.co.uk

ST ANDREWS

The historic university town of St Andrews in Fife is a must visit destination. It has loads to see; golf, a buzzing cafe culture, a castle and a cathedral. More importantly, it has two stunning beaches which can get great surf!.

West Sands is the larger of the two beaches. Well over two kilometres long, it backs on to the world famous Old Course. There is free parking all the way down the beach.

East sands is round the other end of town and has a small car park. It is next to the town's lovely harbour. This helps make East sands more sheltered, so a good bet on windy days.

Surf wise, it works best in medium to big, NE to E swells. Just south of St Andrews is Kingsbarns, a great reef break for more experienced surfers, while north is Tentsmuir, which can be fun when St Andrews is too big.

On a still calm day, a paddle around St Andrew's cliffs is an absolute must, You can paddle between the 2 beaches around the towns one kilometre length of cliffs. There is lots to see, from sea birds to seals, a castle and abbeys silhouette on the cliff tops, and lots of small protruding reefs to maneuver around.

Co-ordinates
West Sands -56.347291,-2.807569
East Sands - 56.336170,-2.781810

Nearest Place
St Andrews, a must see Scottish destination.

Off the Water
St Andrews is the Home of Golf, and with 7 trust run courses and another 40 in the region, it's an almost religious destination for some.

PERTHSHIRE AND THE CENTRAL HIGHLANDS

LOCH LUBHAIR AND LOCH DOCHART

These two Lochs are connected by the River Dochart and make a great Paddling destination, whether on their own or heading to or from the West Coast. They lie next to the A85, one of the main arteries to the West and between Crianlarich and Killin. The largest of the Lochs, Lubhair (pronounced Yoo-ar) has both a layby with parking and the small campsite highlighted in the Co-ordinates. It's a lovely place when the sun shines with some interesting places to see, all under the rounded hills of Breadalbane.

Paddling towards the eastern side of the Loch from the get in, the terrain becomes increasingly wooded and there can be some extremely sheltered water with Lily ponds to admire. If the wind blowing, then this is by far the best place to go for a paddle. Paddling to the west the Loch eventually contracts till it becomes the River Dochart. At low water levels it's possible to paddle upstream to get to Loch Dochart. It is not always possible, too high and the speed of the water is too much to paddle against while too low and some of the corners are too shallow. However, who doesn't like a challenge now and then!.

Co-ordinates
56.406921,-4.55413656.406921,-4.554136

Nearest Place
Killin is Four miles away. With places to eat, stay and the Falls of Dochart to admire (see West Loch Tay for more).

Off the Water

Ben Lawers. Climbing nearby Ben Lawers gives incredible views. Not for the inexperienced, Ben Lawers, at 1214m, is the Highest Perthshire peak and the Highest in the Southern Highlands. Combined on a full on days hike, there are 7 peaks which make up the Ben Lawers range.

LOCH EARN

Loch Earn is a stunning large loch in Mid Scotland. It straddles the border between Stirlingshire and Perthshire, with this it becomes one of the most accessible big Lochs to the cities of Glasgow, Edinburgh, Perth and Stirling. This can therefore be a great location to meet up for a paddle with friends who live in one of the other Scottish Cities to yourself.

It offers grand scenery along all the sides of it's dark water with several Munro's visible, making it a great shout to combine a hike with a paddle. On its Western edge lies the village of Lochearnhead, home of a cracking waterside pub, The Clachan. There are several access points, notably parking in the public car park and walking across the road. Because of the prevailing wind coming from the west, this tends to be the most sheltered area of the loch, making it a popular place with Wakeboarding and Water Ski boats.

Along both edges of the loch are roads, the northern side having the main route, the A85. There are plentiful lay-bys to pull over, park up and get in. The eastern edge of the loch is marked by the lovely village of St Fillans, again with plenty of access points.

Co-ordinates
Lochearnhead - Lochearnhead Public Toilet, Auchraw Terrace, Lochearnhead FK19 8QG,
St Fillans - 56.395371,-4.124794

Nearest place
Lochearnhead and St Fillans both have a pub, shop and places to stay

Off the water

At 985m, Ben Vorlich tower over Loch Earn and the views from the top makes it a worthwhile hike.

LOCH LUBNAIG

Situated in the Trossachs, between Callander and Strathyre, beneath the magnificent peak of Ben Ledi, Loch Lubnaig is a lovely place for a paddle.

It has a shape very much based on its North to South shape, and this, combined with the shelter that Ben Ledi can sometimes provide, means that it can have a lot less wind than many east to west Trossachs lochs in the prevailing wind (Westerly). If the wind is coming from the less dominant North or South directions, then one of the other Lochs in the area will be more suitable, such as Loch Earn or Loch Venachar.

There are several car parks on the main road (A84) providing water side access from your car to the water. It should be noted that the loch is situated in the Loch Lomond and the Trossachs National Park, which has a Bye Law preventing all wild camping.

Co-ordinates
56.277386,-4.283511

Nearest Place
North of the Loch is the small village of Strathyre with a pub and shop, while just south is the tourist hub of Callander with much more facilities.

Off the Water
Ben Ledi offers superb walking and views, the path begins at the Car Park at the Lochs Southern point.

LOCH VENACHER

Loch Venachar lies between the popular tourist town of Callander and the small settlement of Brig o' Turk in the heart of the Loch Lomond and the Trossachs National Park. At 3.7 miles long it offers a big area to explore in a lovely forested landscape. Despite its size it still offers a fair amount of protection from the prevailing wind with plenty of nooks and crannies. The further west you put in, the more calm water you are likely to find.

A good paddle is from the beaches near the Venachar Lochside Cafe on the northern shore (A821) across the Loch to Invertrossachs, which has plenty of secluded beaches and tiny islands to explore.

Portnellan island in Loch Venachar is an Iron Age crannog which is a Scheduled Ancient Monument.

Co-ordinates
56.226335,-4.319391

Nearest Place
Callander is a busy little town with plenty of facilities.

Off the Water
Blair Drummond Safari Park. Just south of Callander this drive through park has plenty of animals to see, including Lions, Elephants and Rhinos.
www.blairdrummond.com

LOCH TAY WEST, KILLIN

Loch Tay is the largest of the Perthshire Lochs and, at its Western end lies Killin.

It's a pretty village with plenty of tourist facilities, chief of which being the majestic Falls of Dochart, a series of rapids which tumble down river and underneath a bridge. This view has to be one of Scotland's most photographed.

Paddle wise, Killin is a great destination. Being surrounded by large hills, they offer protection from the prevailing westerly winds. This can make it a good place to go if the wind is not favourable for Kenmore at its eastern end.

Paddleboarding at Killin is all about contrasts. By getting in, next to the Killin Hotel (park at the Killin Town Hall car park) you start on the Killin canal. This gives ideal, slow moving water to start with, ideal for beginners. As you paddle towards the Loch, under a series of small bridges the terrain opens up with lovely views. An island just before the Loch itself means you can enjoy a leisurely circumnavigation while taking in the views, at the same time not having to fully commit to the more exposed waters of the loch itself. Note that the waters of Loch Tay as you reach it can be extremely shallow for a short distance so there is a chance of getting a deep fin run aground in the soft mud.

Co-ordinates
56.469235,-4.317755

Nearest Place

Killin is a popular village for walkers and tourists. It has plenty of places to stay and eat.

Off the Water

In Killin itself, the River Dochart creates a series of spectacular series of rapids known as the Falls of Dochart. Enjoy a picnic on the banks.

LOCH TAY EAST, KENMORE

Aaaaaah, the sun! How I have missed you! Those golden rays shone down on me as I paddled up Loch Tay this February afternoon. I took the opportunity to blow off my winter cobwebs and have my first British SUP paddle of the year.

Arriving at the stunning conservation village of Kenmore, at Loch Tays eastern edge, I got my gear on and walked my board down to the water's edge. I was greeted by a view of majestic snow capped peaks on the Ben Lawers massif, and best of all, not an iota of wind!. The sun shone down and, reflected by the Loch's waters, the heat given off definitely did not feel like a typical February day.

I set off from the beach and sauntered past the boathouse and through the many buoys sat out on the water, all of them longing for those summer days when the pleasure boats use them for mooring and fill up the bay. The next location for me and my SUP was to paddle over to explore the Isle of Loch Tay.

The Isle of Loch Tay , in Gaelic - Eilean nam Ban-naomh ('Isle of holy women') is about 500 metres away from Kenmore, making a great destination to paddle over to, leave your board at the water's edge, and experience a bit of 'Robinson Crusoe' adventure. The island has a ruin to clamber over, formerly a 12th century nunnery and is the burial place of Queen Sybilla, the wife of Alexander I of Scotland.

My little boy's own adventure over, its back on the water, as I carried on paddling along Loch Tays northern shore, passing the huge hulk of an old boat, sitting forlornly on the shore, as I headed up to Fearnan. The sun was still beating, the mountain views expanded, enabling me to see the snowy mountains which look down on Killin, some 17 miles away. With the prevailing winds behind you, a downwinder from Killin to Kenmore is one the country's best downwind paddles.

It was time to turn around and head towards Kenmore again, and feel the sun's warm rays on my back. I headed diagonally across the loch to its southern edge and the tiny village of Acharn. I scooted around the working salmon farm, past a heron, sat on a buoy, acting like a sentry for the salmon farm.

I then carried along the banks of the Loch to the Scottish Crannog centre. This is an incredible reconstruction of an Iron age dwelling, a Crannog, which sits on stilts above the water. The smoke rising from next to it, was luckily not it going up in flames, but a demonstration of iron age cooking and crafts.

The final leg is upon me as the waters become shallower and I make my way back to Kenmores beach. I find it hard to leave this beautiful place to put my gear away, savouring the views and the sun. But I am thankful I got to have such a stunning paddle, only a SUP lets me experience this place like this

Co-ordinates
56.584337,-3.997700

Nearest Place
Kenmore has a shop, several places to eat, drink and stay. Aberfeldy with a bigger selection is 6 miles away.

Off the Water
Scottish Crannog Centre. A Crannog is a stilted homestead over a loch and was used 2500 plus years ago. Step back in time in this reconstructed Crannog with plenty of hands on things to do.
www.crannog.co.uk

SCOTTISH SUP GUIDE

LOCH RANNOCH

Beautiful Loch Rannoch is a fairly remote loch but with easy roadside access. It has stunning views looking west into Glencoe and of Schiehallion, 'the fairy mountain'. Kinloch Rannoch is a small village on the eastern shore of the loch, it has several hotels, a cafe and a petrol pump, the 'buzzing' hub of local Rannoch life. You can park right by the water's edge and get straight onto the water here, or carry on driving to the western side of the loch at Rannoch station, just stop and get on wherever looks good.

While on the drive up from the A9 and Pitlochry (its one road in, one road out round here folks), you will pass two other lochs which can be paddled. Loch Tummel and Dunalastair Water. Dunalastair is a good bet on a windy day, when a SUP may be a mission on Loch Rannoch, due to its shallow waters and sheltered location. Loch Tummel has similar stunning views like Rannoch, the easiest access points are to be found at the campsite you pass just after Queens View visitor centre, or take the (even) quieter road along the lochs southern shore, where the Hydro dam and the Sailing club are good bets.

Co-ordinates
56.699993,-4.193792

Nearest Place
Kinloch Rannoch has a shop and a few places to eat and drink.

Off the Water
Craigh Na Dun is the stone circle used in the TV series 'Outlander' where Claire goes back in time. They are just outside Kinloch

Rannoch.

LOCH TUMMEL

Loch Tummel is situated west of the popular tourist town of Pitlochry, which is the nearest spot with major facilities. It is one of the most photographed views of Scotland with the view taken from the Queen's View visitor centre being highlighted on plenty of visitor guides and postcards.

It's a big narrow body of water to paddle on, running west from Tummel Bridge toward the East and Clunie Hydro Electric Power Station. Access wise, the smaller southern road offers the best, with a few small roadside lay-bys, especially near the power station itself. This area offers both a wee bit of wind protection as well as several small islands to head out and explore as well.

Co-ordinates
56.719134,-3.824742

Nearest Place
Pitlochry is a major tourist town about 6 miles from the eastern edge of Loch Tummel. It has plenty of places to stay, eat, drink and shop.

Off the Water
From Queens View Visitor Centre, sitting high above the Loch is one of the most photographed views in the country.
https://forestryandland.gov.scot/visit/forest-parks/tay-forest-park/queens-view-visitor-centre

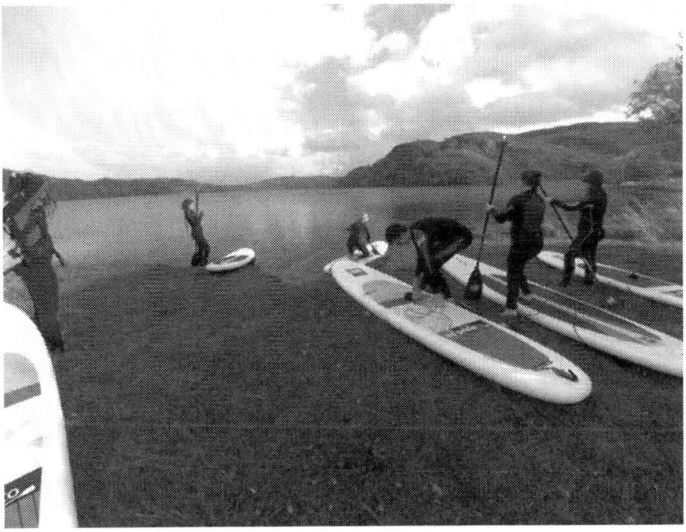

CLUNIE LOCH

Halfway between Dunkeld and Blairgowrie sits Clunie Loch, one of Perthshire's most popular Paddle Boarding locations. With easy access from car to water and surrounded by hills and trees, it is one of the areas most weatherproof paddle spots. With the prevailing winds coming from the West, the laybys or church side parking on this side usually offer the most calm waters to explore.

Clunie is blessed with its own Island, upon which stands the ruins of a 15th Century Castle. Although crumbling (and unsafe to use the non existent stairs to upper levels), it's still an amazing place to spend some time, the Laird of your own private island.

With Lily Ponds in the Summer on its Western edge, gentle shoreline and limited access to pretty much the entire Northern shore, it has plenty of Wildlife to enjoy. Recently a pair of Ospreys has taken to nesting in one of its trees, an amazing sight.

Clunie has become a popular camping spot and with this litter has become a problem. We would encourage all visitors to take their litter home with them and help keep access open to this special place.

Co-ordinates
Clunie Parish Church, Clunie, Blairgowrie PH10 6RQ

Nearest Place
Clunie Loch is 5 miles from the town of Dunkeld (and 8 miles from Dunkeld). Both have lots of facilities and have lovely Riverside walks.

Off the Water
Learn the art of paddling an ancient watercraft, the Coracle on Clunie Loch.
www.outdoorexplore.co.uk

RIVER ISLA, COUPAR ANGUS

Flowing gently through farmland, yet with views to the distant Angus Glens and Perthshire hills, the River Isla makes a great trip. Getting on the Isla just underneath the small town of Coupar Angus, it is a nice fairly gentle run as the Isla sedately makes its way to the end of its journey as it joins the River Tay.

The best place to egress this section of the Isla is by the A93 at Kinclaven. This trip of about 7 miles is a lovely touring section. It is worth noting that the Prevailing wind is likely to be blowing into your face, so worth doing on a day when the wind is less strong.

Co-ordinates
Get on - 56.548492,-3.279548
Get off - 56.528186,-3.361759

Nearest Place
Coupar Angus, by the get in, is a small town with a supermarket and several places to eat.

Off the Water
Meikleour Beech Hedge. Just a short walk from the get off is this imposing shaped Beech Tree Hedge. It is in the Guinness Book of Records as the World's biggest.

SCOTTISH SUP GUIDE

ADVENTUROUS PERTHSHIRE LOCHS - BIKE OR HIKE TO A HIDDEN GEM

Perthshire is blessed with some incredible places to paddle, waterside parking, good facilities and easy, legal access. What it also has, in abundance are many lesser known Lochs. Places which are not as easily accessible yet reward the intrepid with solitude, magnificent views and a sense of achievement in even getting to them. With a bike or a hike in, the Lochs below are all magical places for those wanting a real, away from it all place to Paddleboard.

Loch Skiach - In the hills above Logierait and Ballinguard, up from the B898 (Dunkeld to Aberfeldy), Loch Skiach (and its neighbour Little Loch Skiach) is a 5km hike or ride in. With views across to Ben Vrackie and down to the River Tay, it is a fantastic place for a paddle away from it all. The highlight of Loch Skiach as well as the Paddling reward is the fact that it has it's very own Bothy. An overnight stay, or just as a spot to prepare some well deserved lunch, this is a very unique place to make the effort to Paddleboard.

Co-ordinates
Loch - 56.604706,-3.710655
Leave the car here - 56.630739,-3.662171

Loch Ordie - Situated high up on the opposite side of the Tay Valley from Loch Skiach and can be accessed from paths from both Dunkeld and Guay. It's a very pretty, decent sized Loch. On one (long and best suited to bike) route in from Dunkeld, it is possible to Paddleboard on Four different Locations; Ordie, Rotmell, Dowally and Mill Dam.

Co-ordinates
Loch - 56.629691,-3.582405

Leave the car here - 56.626879,-3.621260

Loch Kennard - Sat in the middle of the Griffin Forest, high above Aberfeldy sits Loch Kennard. A beautiful, large, tree lined Loch accessed by Forest roads from the car park on the A826. Indeed the Car Park is next to the small but very paddle-able Loch Na Creige.

Co-ordinates
Loch - 56.592972,-3.789005

Leave the car here - Griffin Forest Car Park, Aberfeldy PH8 0EB

RIVER TUMMEL - PITLOCHRY TO BALLINLUIG

This is a great section of about 5 miles of fairly fast grade one to two water of lovely countryside. This is the final stretch of the River Tummel before it joins the mighty River Tay. It starts in Pitlochry, a major Highland tourist town, with great facilities including hotels, hostels, campsites, cafes and shops. The route starts just below the huge, impressive, Faskally hydro-electric dam (note, this river is dam released, so be aware of the water levels rising when on the water). Above the dam is lovely Loch Faskally which makes another great destination

Parking at the start is possible near the Pitlochry festival theatre which has a car park, or the Port-Na-Craig hamlet road. Alternatively, park by the rugby pitch on the opposite bank.

From the start you are in fast flowing water, before a nice calm section heading underneath Pitlochry's foot and road bridges. The river then begins to become a little more shallow just before the road bridge for the A9. After picking your line down here (left at low water levels) and heading under the bridge, the first rapid awaits. As with all the rapids on this section it is a nice, safe wave train. At medium to high levels it is a lot of fun to surf it too.

Heading down towards Ballinluig, lots of fun lines and small rapids await. Just watch out for anglers and overhanging branches on the outside of some bends.

The egress point for this section is just before the next road bridge on the right hand side at Ballinluig. Alternatively, you can carry on the 9 miles to Dunkeld to make a fantastic fully day on the water

Co-ordinates
Get on (Parking) - 56.701320,-3.739703
Get on (River) - 56.698673,-3.736620
Get Off - 56.649839,-3.671243

Nearest Place
Pitlochry is a popular tourist town with lots going on, places to stay, eat and shop.

Off the Water
Canyoning. Nearby at the Falls of Bruar, the drops, slides and waterfalls make it one of the best Canyoning venues in the country.
www.thecanyoningcompany.co.uk

RIVER TAY, DUNKELD, PERTHSHIRE

The River Tay is Scotland's longest river, flowing from stunning Loch Tay all the way to the sea in Dundee. Most sections are safe and easy for SUPs. The Grandtully whitewater section should be portaged, while the section between Stanley and Thistlebrig should only be undertaken by experienced whitewater SUP'ers.

The River around the charming twin villages of Dunkeld and Birnam passes stunning scenery and historic monuments, such as the ruins of Dunkeld Cathedral and the Birnam Oak, as mentioned in Shakespeare's Macbeth. The river is usually a fairly easy paddle for all abilities, with great views of the tree lined valley. Just upstream from the Hilton hotel on the river right, there is sometimes a nice play wave to surf your board in, with deep, safe water downstream of it.

As you go through Dunkeld, the gradient increases as it heads underneath the Thomas Telford designed bridge. There are navigable wave trains (either standing up or kneeling down, depending on how wet you want to get!) on both the left and right hand banks, the right hand bank usually having a bigger, bouncier wave train.

There are lots of places to access the river. For a long day paddle, get on at the Logierait Inn (Logierait) or Port-Na-Craig Inn (Pitlochry). For a shorter trip, a footpath just by the Dalguise road turning off the A9, leads down to a big river eddy.

Egress can be done in low flows just above the Telford Bridge in

Dunkeld, or otherwise, below the wave trains on the River's right hand bank.

There's lots to see and do in Dunkeld and Birnam....the Beatrix Potter exhibition and garden, Loch of the Lowes Osprey colony, Hermitage waterfall, mountain biking, 4x4 safaris, quad biking, pubs, restaurants and cafes.

Co-ordinates
Get on - 56.649839,-3.671243
Get off -56.561777,-3.577611

Nearest Place
The twin Villages of Dunkeld and Birnam are among the prettiest in Scotland. They have plenty of places to stay, eat and shop. There are no facilities in Caputh, but nearby Murthly has a shop and a restaurant.

Off the Water
Loch of the Lowe's. A Scottish success story, Ospreys have been reintroduced to the area and you can view these magnificent creatures just outside Dunkeld.
https://scottishwildlifetrust.org.uk/reserve/loch-of-the-lowes/

MATT GAMBLES

RIVER TAY - DUNKELD TO CAPUTH

The River Tay is Scotland's longest river, snaking its way through stunning terrain along its length. This section is 3 miles long and marks the divide between the Highlands and Lowlands, passing over the Highland fault line. Starting in Dunkeld, you can get on at the Atholl Arms, which is a Scottish Canoe Association access point - this puts you straight into a small rapid, nothing of consequence though, fun to do standing up or on your knees.

To avoid the rapid, you can enter the river at the other side in the village of Birnam which has access via lots of small beaches. From here down you go past lots of sweeping turns as you head down to Caputh. The views upstream are especially spectacular, looking up to Dunkelds steep, craggy valley.

The get out point on this section is the road bridge in Caputh, which you cannot miss, as you see it from a kilometre upstream.

Co-ordinates
Get On - 56.561777,-3.577611
Get Off - 56.539160,-3.483129

Nearest Place
The twin Villages of Dunkeld and Birnam are among the prettiest in Scotland. They have plenty of places to stay, eat and shop. There are no facilities in Caputh, but nearby Murthly has a shop and a restaurant.

Off the Water
One of the most popular Mountain Biking destinations, there is something for everyone, from gnarly Downhills to gentle forest tracks.

www.progressionbikesscotland.com

RIVER TAY - STANLEY TO THISTLEBRIG - WHITEWATER

North of the City of Perth, and just off the main North to South artery, the A9 lies the small village of Stanley. The mighty River Tay flows next to it and its normal, flat but fast flowing nature changes. The River changes its attitude and appearance, providing some really fun and SUP friendly Grade 2 to 3 Whitewater. Being a River in a Country with a well earned reputation for rain, levels can change dramatically here, with different features working at different times.

From the get in at the bottom of the single track Linn Road, it looks like most of the Rivers length, lacking rapids. However, look upstream and you can see a small, fun rapid, a great rapid to find your feet before paddling downstream. You can either walk up the river bank, cross a small stream of water on the left and carry on hiking up, or ferry glide over to the central island on the River and walk upstream to enter the rapid.

Above this rapid is a much larger rapid called Campsie Linn. A large amount of water flows through and makes some huge whirlpools and boils. It is highly recommended to stay away from the Linn and not paddle it.

Paddling downstream from the get in and around the corner, a River wide Weir becomes visible with, at low to medium levels, three open sections to take. The Middle section is the deepest and the recommended line through. At higher levels the water may be going over the entire weir, you can see this Middle section channel still as it will have the longest wave train coming out the downstream side of it.

The Weir produces a fantastic wave for the nimble Paddle Boarder at very low River levels.

After the Weir, there are several sections of smaller Grade 2 rapids, with plenty of eddies to pick up the pieces in between.

The final rapid is called Thistlebrig, a fun, bouncy long wave train. The Exit point is on the River Right bank directly after this, whereupon you can walk your board up a long set of steps to the Thistlebrig Car Park. Just after the egress point, at High River levels, again on River Right, is Wee Eric, a fantastic Surf Wave. One of Scotland's best River Surfing waves, it's a mellow ride, with an eddy right next to it.

As always with Whitewater Paddle Boarding make sure that you have the correct skills, equipment and experience before heading out.

Co-ordinates
Get in - 56.487311,-3.431786
Get out - 56.471630,-3.449397
Get out parking - 1 Perth Rd, Stanley, Perth PH1 4NF

Nearest Place
Stanley is a small village, but it has a cafe, small shop and a few pubs. For more facilities, the City of Perth is just down the road.

Off the Water
Stanley Mills. You will pass this impressive complex from the Industrial Revolution on your paddle down the River. It is open as a visitor attraction with plenty of hands-on exhibits about it's history.
https://www.historicenvironment.scot/visit-a-place/places/stanley-mills/

SCOTTISH SUP GUIDE

LOCH FREUCHIE AND THE RIVER QUAICH, PERTHSHIRE

River Quaich

This lovely little river feeds into Loch Freuchie, so a great day can be had exploring the two. At Loch Freuchies far western end, underneath a little stone humpback bridge, the River Quaich meanders into the Loch. By putting in here (and with a bit of a stoop to get under the bridge), you can enjoy a stunning paddle up the river, as far as you want to go (weather dependent). It meanders back and forth, so it is very slow moving, and has a fantastic exploration feel about it.

Loch Freuchie

Paddling on Loch Freuchie really is about getting away from it all. It's a fairly remote Loch, equidistant between Dunkeld, Aberfeldy and Crieff (all between 10 and 12 miles away). Loch Freuchie (Gaelic - Fraoch - 'the heatherly loch') offers stunning views of the Breadalbane mountains and a real feeling of getting away from it all. It's also only a few kilometres in length, making it perfect for a circumnavigation. Why not, bring along a picnic so you can stop along one of its beaches too?.

Paddling from the get in to the East and the main part of the Loch, there is a small island (a man made Crannog). Legend has it, a man called Fraoch went to the Dragon inhabited Island at the request of a maiden to collect Rowan Berries. Evading the Dragon he brought the berries back, the maiden then said she desired the Rowan Tree itself. This time he woke the Dragon who in a fight, gnawed off his legs and arms, will we ever find out if the legend is true or not?.

Access to the water is probably easiest from the Loch's western end, just off a private road leading to a small humpback bridge. Take extra care and consideration while finding a spot to leave your car. To find Loch Freuchie, take the road signposted 'Glen Quaich' of the A822 in the small settlement of Amulree.

Co-ordinates
56.521630,-3.864560

Nearest Place
Loch Freuchie is near the tiny settlement of Amulree, from here it is equidistant to the town's of Aberfeldy, Crieff and Dunkeld. All are about 12 miles away and have plenty of facilities.

Off the Water
Both Crieff and Aberfeldy are home to World famous Whiskies. There are excellent distillery tours and tastings available at both.
Dewars, Aberfeldy https://www.dewars.com/gl/en/aberfeldydistillery/
GlenTurret, Crieff https://theglenturret.com/pages/age-verification?r=https://theglenturret.com/

MATT GAMBLES

ABERDEEN AND THE NORTH EAST

NAIRN

Nairn in Moray is a lovely seaside town in the county of Moray, fairly near to the Highland capital of Inverness. It offers plenty of facilities including cafes, shops, campsites and hotels, with lovely beachside parks to relax in.

Nairn has miles and miles of sandy beach to paddle alongside, going both east and west from the Harbour. The views from the water are spectacular, looking across the Moray Firth to the Black Isle and the Caithness coast beyond. The chances of seeing a pod of inquisitive, playful Dolphins is fairly high and definitely a big draw to the area. Another is the claim that Nairn has to be the sunniest place in mainland Scotland.

At the centre of it all is Nairn Harbour, which is a great place to find your balance in flat, still water, exploring the moored boats, before paddling into the lower River Nairn, which leads down onto the Moray Firth itself. If the weather is against you, then the Harbour means that you can still get out for a paddle in sheltered conditions.

Co-ordinates
Harbour Car Park, 140 Harbour St, Nairn IV12 4PH

Nearest Place
Nairn is a popular holiday resort with all the facilities you would ever need.

Off the Water
Culloden Battlefield, the moving site of the last pitched battle on British soil. The informative Visitor Centre will help you make

sense of it.
https://www.nts.org.uk/visit/places/culloden

HOPEMAN

Hopeman is a lovely seaside village in Moray. It has a fantastic, welcoming caravan park, plenty of eateries and art galleries, stunning coastal paths, twee beach huts (very instagrammable!) and a skatepark.

It has a large, double basin harbour as its centerpiece, meaning at Mid to High Tide, you can paddle in most conditions in a decent size area in most conditions. It is a great place to explore.
Leaving the harbour mouth, you enter the smaller of Hopeman's two beaches, East Sands. It's a lovely spot to paddle with spectacular views towards the Black Isle and beyond. Sometimes the surf gods play ball and you will find the most beginner friendly of Hopeman's surf spots here.

At the other side of the Harbour is the larger West Sands, a series of sandy bays, with rocky islets here and there to pick your way through. The most western edge has the finest sands and a series of beautiful Beach Huts to admire. There is car parking at the Harbour and by the West Sands. By combining a harbour start, into the east sands and round to the west sands, with the wind behind you, you can enjoy a downwinder then walk back along the road to your vehicle quite easily.

Co-ordinates
57.710266,-3.436478

Nearest Place
Hopeman is a small resort and fishing village. It has a campsite, shops, places to stay, eat and drink.

Off the Water

Hopeman Skatepark is just by the East Beach in the village's large park. With a mini ramp and a street course, it is a great place to ride.

LOSSIEMOUTH

Known as the 'Jewel of the Moray Firth', Lossiemouth is a lovely seaside resort with a variety of places to go Paddleboarding. Lossie, as it is known, has plenty of facilities, with high quality golf courses, excellent local Ice Cream and an active Air Force base to top it off. The town itself sits on small cliffs in between its two beaches, each offering different paddling options.

The more sheltered West Beach is the best place for a gentle paddle and an explore. It has a large, gently sloping beach mixed with rocks and cliffs for three miles, all the way to Covesea Lighthouse. Offshore, and in the right conditions (and experience), the Halliman Skerries with its old Lighthouse is an obvious Paddling target. Underneath Covesea lighthouse itself, and with parking near to the Lighthouse, the beach gets more surf usually, being more exposed than West Beach.

Round the other side of Lossie is the West Beach is usually accessed by a pedestrian walkway over the tidal River Lossie. This has recently condemned meaning access to the mile upon mile of glorious sand backed by dunes is currently off limits to almost everyone. For the Paddleboarder, this is not a problem however as you can paddle the short distance over to the beach, or wade across on the low tide. Be careful with this however as the water can be fast flowing around the Bridge stanchions. Once on the beach you will be rewarded with miles of empty beach and lots of potential surf breaks. Lossiemouth is one of the main Surfing centres on the Moray coast, yet there are plenty of peaks so crowds will never be a problem.

Being in the Moray Firth, it is a Wildlife Spotters dream with Dolphins and maybe even Orca Whales to be admired.

Co-ordinates
West Beach - West Beach Car Park, St Gerardine Rd, Lossiemouth IV31 6SR
East Beach - Seatown, Lossiemouth IV31 6JJ

Nearest Place
Lossiemouth is a popular tourist town with facilities to match. Excellent Golf opportunities abound.

Off the Water
The Findhorn Foundation. Near to Lossiemouth, this is a very unique community. A spiritual, holistic eco village with a vibrant array of events, crafts and more.
www.findhorn.org

ARGYLL AND THE GREAT GLEN

ARISAIG

Azure blue waters, white sand beaches, dolphins skipping by...the Caribbean Sea right?.....think again, this is the West Coast of Scotland. Arisaig and its next door neighbour, the Silver Sands of Morar. They are situated at the end of the Road to the Isles, the A830 from Fort William, the drive in itself is a Scottish highlight, passing through magnificent scenery (including the GlenFinnan Memorial and the Train Viaduct made famous in Harry Potter).

Arisaig consists of a number of small white sand bays with laybys to park in. The winds usually come from the West and are therefore onshore so less worries about being blown to sea than most places. Still, it is essential to be well prepared and competent with a high tidal range here.

The views are as spectacular as the colour of the water beneath your feet, looking out towards the islands of Rum and Eigg. In the right conditions, a sunset paddle here could give you some of the most Instagrammable shots in the World!.

Co-ordinates
56.945756,-5.854667

Nearest Place
Mallaig, 8 miles away, is a pretty little working harbour and ferry port. It has a small supermarket amongst it's facilities.

Off the Water
Take a Whale and Seal watching trip with local operators.
www.arisaig.co.uk

MATT GAMBLES

SANNA BAY

For a truly Off the Beaten Track Stand Up Paddleboarding destination, Sanna Bay is right up there. This is the Most Westerly point of the UK Mainland and consists of 4 beaches of varying sizes. All of them offer white sands, turquoise waters and very likely, the place to yourselves. The views are magnificent, looking out from the tip of the Ardnamurchan Peninsula towards the Small Isles of Rum, Eigg, Muck and Canna, sometimes with Dolphins and Whales to be seen in the foreground. The bay hopping, rock pools and incredible views make for some great Paddle trips, in a Southerly or South Westerly, there can also be some pretty solid surf to be found.

Co-ordinates
56.745381,-6.175346

Nearest Place
Sanna is pretty out there. It is along single track roads at the end of the Ardnamurchan Peninsula, reached from either the A830 near Glenfinnan or the ferry from Corran. Both of these then involve long single track journeys, though both through incredible scenery. Treat the journey as an experience to savour as much as the destination itself. Strontian and Acharacle both have tiny shops, with a few small places to stay dotted around. Fort William is the nearest sizable town with all facilities.

Off the Water
Ardnamurchan Distillery. Take a tour of this award winning Whiskey Distillery in Acharacle.
https://www.visitscotland.com/info/see-do/ardnamurchan-

MATT GAMBLES

distillery-p1202051

GLENCOE, LOCH LEVEN

Imposing Mountains surround Loch Leven by the small village of Glencoe. With magnificent views, incredible views and Wildlife spotting, it is an excellent place to Paddleboard.

At the Get in, just outside the village of Ballachulish and by the Isles of Glencoe there are bays either side of the Hotel complex meaning that if conditions are not favourable for one then get in or off at the other.

This is a sea loch so access will be better at Mid to High tide. The views from the water are incredible, looking up into the famous Pass of Glencoe and imposing Mountains in all directions.

The area was the Battlefield of the infamous Massacre of Glencoe of 1692. There is an excellent Visitor Centre to learn more about it. The small group of Islands which you can see and paddle to on the Loch contains the Island of Eilean Munde, which is a Clan burial site. Used for Hundreds of years it contains many graves of those killed in the massacre. A unique and eerie place to Paddle to, please be respectful when landing and spending time here.

Co-ordinates
56.680226,-5.132401

Nearest Place
The get in is by the large Isles of Glencoe Hotel complex and next to the village of Ballachulish which has a shop, toilets and places to stay. Nearby Glencoe also has more places to eat , stay, a shop and a garage.

Off the Water

An essential trip, take a drive through the Pass of Glencoe. This road, through the glen winds up towards the plateaux of Rannoch Moor, taking in steep mountains, vertical cliffs and surging waterfalls along the way. Regularly used in film and television, including Skyfall and Harry Potter, it is one of the Scottish Bucket list road trips.

KERRERA

Just south of Oban, a few hundred metres across the Firth of Lorn from the mainland, lies Kerrera. This island is a World away from the hustle of the port, fishing and tourist bustle in Oban. It. It is a fantastic destination to head via Paddleboard and explore it's lovely shoreline both on foot as well as board.

The paddle across starts from the same small landing ramp as the tiny Kerrera Ferry. This also means you could use this Ferry if required for one of the legs of your trip. The paddle across is on the sea and the tide can rush in and out of the Forth, so do consider the tide times beforehand.

It's a nice paddle across with fantastic views to the North towards Oban and Benderloch, to the South, the Small Isles. On Kerrera itself there are plenty of small paths, one of which leads to the South and the ruins of Gylen Castle. The North of the Island houses a tiny marina and a fish farm, so there is plenty to see from the water. Pods of Dolphins can regularly be seen, especially when they follow a Ferry or large Fishing boat arriving into Oban.

Co-ordinates
Mainland start point - 56.397130,-5.509779

Nearest Place
Oban is two miles North is the main Ferry port for trips to the Islands of Scotland's West Coast. As such it is packed full of places to stay, eat and shop. Several of the Islands, including Mull and Lismore make easy day trips, even if you don't plan on exploring them for longer. Just by the Ferry ramp is a large Campsite at Gallanach as well as the Puffin Diving Centre, for fans of underwater

adventure.

Off the Water

Head on a Ferry to the Isles. There are plenty of amazing places to choose from; Picture postcard Tobermory on Mull, Religious splendour on Iona, or the smaller and less known Lismore or Colonsay. There are the white sand beaches and surf of Tiree and Coll and even further afield, the rugged and spectacular Outer Hebrides.

https://www.calmac.co.uk/

CASTLE STALKER

A fan of Monty Python? Love Castles and Islands? This Paddle destination could well be for you. In Monty Python and the Holy Grail, the 'Castle of Aaaargh' where the Grail supposedly resides is actually Castle Stalker. Situated on a tiny Island just off the coast of the tidal Loch Linnhe on the West Coast, near Appin and not too far from the town of Oban.

The paddle out to Castle Stalker is fairly easy, as the Island is in a pretty sheltered bay, which becomes apparent by the amount of small boats moored around it. The Loch is tidal and the bay is muddy and not very accessible at Low tide so do take this into account.

The Castle (originally built in the mid 1400's) and it's silhouette is extremely photogenic yet the scenery around is equally spectacular. In good weather it is possible to use the bay as a starting point for longer trips, especially the Isles of Shuma of Lismore, which is a lovely spot to explore.

The Island and Castle are privately owned so please do not land unless you have booked a private guided tour.

Co-ordinates
56.570473,-5.378422

Nearest Place
There is a cafe on the A828 overlooking the Island, while nearby Appin has basic facilities. For more head to Oban, which is a much bigger town with plenty going on.

MATT GAMBLES

LOCH NESS

The Big Daddy of all Scottish Lochs, and one that will be on many a Paddleboarders tick list. Even if you do not manage to catch a glimpse of the Fabled Loch Ness Monster, the views are pretty awe inspiring anyway.

Loch Ness is huge, extending for 23 miles (37km) from Fort Augustus in the West towards the Highland Capital, Inverness in the East. It has a multitude of places to access the water from along both its Northern and Southern sides, some of note being at Fort Augustus, Dores and the many lay bys on the Northern side (A82) as the road reaches the Eastern edge of the Loch.

Because of its size, the weather makes a huge impact on conditions. Indeed with 27 miles of fetch, the Author has SUP Surfed here, experiencing 4 ft Windswell on a rocky and somewhat sketchy point break break setup. Be aware of all conditions and make sure you are fully prepared and experienced if you do decide to SUP on Loch Ness.

Having said that, with the right conditions, then the views are spectacular and it really is a Bucket List Paddle. Winds tend to come from the West so it is usually calmer at Fort Augustus in the West. The small marina just outside, on the A82 heading towards Inverness is a pretty good weather proof entry point with Cherry Island in the middle of the bay plus the Historic Caledonian Canal locks to admire as well as the Loch views themselves.

Co-ordinates

North Loch Ness - Parking Loch Ness, Inverness IV3 8LA
Dores 57.382478,-4.333125
Cherry Island Marina 57.154779,-4.674169

Nearest Place
Inverness is near to both the eastern get ons, the Highland Capital is the biggest and busiest place for hours around so you can stock up on whatever is required.
Fort Augustus in the west is much smaller, but, a popular tourist stop, has plenty of facilities.

Off the Water
The big Riverside Park in Inverness, Bught Park is home to one of the UK'S best outdoor Skateparks and Pumptracks. With free entry and a fantastic location it's well worth a visit.

LOCH MORLICH

With a large sandy beach to enjoy, there is somewhat of a coastal vibe, highlighted by the fact that it is the only Freshwater beach to have a coveted Keep Scotland Beautiful Beach Award. Yet, at 320m high above sea level and backed by the magnificent Northern Cairngorm Mountains, this Loch, just above the town of Aviemore has more than meets the eye.

In the Springtime indeed it is more than possible to go for a Paddle on this stunning Loch and then mere minutes later be Skiing down a run at nearby Cairngorm Ski Resort. The view from the water across the beach and up to Cairngorm is a Scottish classic. There is car parking, refreshments and easy access from the beach side of the Loch.

The area less visited on the Loch by Paddlers is the Western edge, the first part of the Loch you see as you approach from Aviemore. With car parking in several laybys next to the Loch, this is usually the side of the loch with the calmest waters to paddle as the wind pushes across the loch towards the beachside.

Co-ordinates
Beach - 57.168145,-3.701002
Sailing club area - 57.165468,-3.722860

Nearest Place
Next to the Loch is by the tiny settlement of Glenmore which has two cafes and a large campsite. For lots more places to eat, shop and stay, head back down the road to Aviemore.

Off the Water

In the late spring, combine your Paddle with a Ski or Snowboard at Cairngorm mountain Ski resort. Hire is readily available with plenty of pistes and spectacular views.
www.cairngormmountain.co.uk

THE NORTHERN HIGHLANDS AND THE NORTH COAST 500

THE NORTH COAST 500 - A PADDLEBOARD GUIDE TO THE ULTIMATE ROAD TRIP

The far north of Scotland is wild, rugged and untamed. Its a real 'out there' destination where you can get away from the rat race, and discover your own piece of SUP nirvana. In the last few weeks I have undertaken two SUP road trips to this incredible region. Staying in a van, with boards on the roof, myself and a fellow SUP surfer, Rich, were to find a land virtually untapped with potential for SUP'ing .

Roads narrow up here, houses are few and far apart (think miles and miles apart) and every car that you pass you find yourself giving a friendly wave to...simple pleasures in a grand landscape.Being as unpopulated as it is, the chances of being in the water (let alone on the beach), it really feels like you are the first paddle boarder to surf or paddle that spot, and in many cases, it will be the truth.

So, if vast landscapes, exploration and peace and quiet appeal, then Scotland's far north could be the place for you. The weather here is extremely fickle so you may find that the 1 ft surf forecast on magic seaweed turns out to be 40 mile winds and 10 ft monster swells.....the trick up here is to be able to change your initial plans if needed and go with the flow. There are beaches and coves that can work in most conditions, so if your initial spot is blown out, check the map and drive on. Inland you will find lots of majestic lochs and rivers, where odds are you will be the first SUP to hit the water ever (the roads from Bonar bridge and Lairg to Durness or Tongue, will get you into places with incredible touring potential.

Back on the coast, Oldmoreshore (near Kinlochbervie) on the west coast is easily accessible to get to and is a beautiful sheltered beach which can get some great surf in tropical looking waters. If it's flat then the touring and exploring opportunities are endless.

Sandwood bay is a very remote beach further on, which involves several hours walk in to it (inflatables could be the way forward here), but the rewards are incredible views and camping potential. It is said that if it is flat at Sandwood, then everywhere in Scotland will be.

Driving up the west coast, we reach the north coast at the straggled coastal village of Durness. It has accommodation,two shops and two pubs...a real metropolis up here, so make sure you stock up on provisions. It has three surf beaches, Balnakeil, Sango Bay and Sango Beg. They all face different directions so can hoover up any swell going. On our last trip, Balnakeil was flat as a pancake while Sango Beg was firing. All the beaches are in majestic surroundings as well, so make sure you get the chance to SUP in the far north west of Scotland.

Driving east from Durness, the single track road is slow going, but the unbelievable scenery certainly makes up for that, the grand landscapes of Loch Eriboll enticing you onto the water. Towards Tongue and Talmine, there is again real SUP exploration potential, especially out to the Rabbit Islands.

Driving on, the next little village is Bettyhill, which houses two incredible beaches, Farr Bay and Armadale. These can hold a hell of a lot of surf and have great access. You can check the surf from the roadside and they are a great place to surf and are sheltered from the prevailing winds, which can be a godsend.

Carrying on driving westwards, Melvich is a river mouth break that can be fantastic, just watch for rips. The Nuclear reactor at Dounreay looms over the coast next, best to avoid the beaches in its vicinity!.

After Dounreay, the landscape changes dramatically as we leave the county of Sutherland and enter Caithness. The land is flatter, characterized by stone slabs in the fields as stone walls, and the opportunities for surf change too. Caithness is the home of world class waves breaking onto shallow reefs. Beaches are at a premium, so make sure your surfing is up to scratch as it can be board (and bone) breaking territory. It's certainly worth taking time to visit the mythical waves of Brims Ness, Shit Pipe and Thurso East, you may get to see pro surfers tear them to shreds (or themselves to shreds if it goes wrong!).

Thurso is the main (and indeed, only) town on the north coast, so it's time to stock up on supplies, check out the mighty Thurso East and get used to seeing traffic lights, Tesco and people again.

Leaving Thurso, we continue east towards John O' Groats.

On the way, Dunnet Beach is one of only a few beaches in Caithness and after frothing on watching the pro's in Thurso, you can get on the water in safe conditions and a bit of surf. John O' Groats, valhalla for sponsored walkers, is where the north coast ends and the east coast begins.

Just outside John O' Groats, a small side road leads to Duncansby Stacks. Here, 200ft high cliffs drop into the North Sea and three equally huge cliff stacks lie just off the coast. Initially here just to admire the views, we found glassy conditions on the water. With a twinkle in our eyes, we both said how incredible it would be if we could find a way down the cliffs and go out on our boards. Upon further inspection, we found a steep but doable path down to the water. The decision was made, this was too good an opportunity to miss, so we geared up and scrambled down the cliff (inflatables are highly recommended). Onto the water, and with skuas and puffins flying about us, we got a unique view of this amazing landscape. If any other stand up paddlers have also had the honour of doing this before us, I would be very surprised.

Buzzing after the Duncansby Stack paddle, it's time to drive south to Sinclairs Bay, just north of Wick. It is a huge crescent shaped beach which has access at both ends of the beach. At the south end, and by the grand Ackergill Tower we got to surf some nice 3 foot swell.

The surf didn't stop there and a few hours south the beach break at Brora served up more juice for us. Tired and exhausted, it was time to put the pedal to the metal for the long drive home. The far north of Scotland again delivered with great surf, an unspoilt, varied landscape and the knowledge that I have to return to this amazing place.

GAIRLOCH

Gairloch in the North West Highlands is as spectacular a place to SUP as they come, boasting white sand beaches, islands, incredible wildlife and views. Reached by stunning drive from the Highland's capital, Inverness, Gairloch is a village spread out around several bays, from the harbour and north to the Big Sands Caravan Park. All types of accommodation are available plus several pubs, eateries and galleries. The community run GALE Centre is a great first place to visit with local information, good food and amazing views.

Depending on conditions, there are several places to Paddleboard, the one thing that unites them is incredible views. The busy Harbour can offer the best sheltered paddleboarding, especially from Mid to High Tide. Just north on the coastal road, parking near the golf course, you come to Gairloch main beach. This offers incredible white sands and clear blue waters. Several rock escarpments and coves can be explored from here.

North again comes Big Sands Beach, next to the caravan park of the same name. As the name suggests, there are plenty of white sands to admire and stunning vistas. Offshore is Longa Island, with the requisite experience and conditions at hand this can be an amazing day trip out to it.

Wildlife abounds with dolphin sightings likely and a chance of spotting whales, several whale watching companies are based in Gairloch.

Co-ordinates
Harbour 57.711065,-5.683140

Main Beach 57.716678,-5.683118
Big Sands 57.734154,-5.764347

Nearest Place
Gairloch has plenty of facilities in this little seaside resort

Off the Water
Take a Dolphin Spotting Boat from the Harbour. Dolphins, Orca Whales and much more can regularly be seen.

BADACHRO

Situated on the banks of Loch Gairloch, a few miles from Gairloch itself, lies the lovely hamlet of Badachro. Badachro is situated in a sheltered cove which enables it to be a great destination to Paddle from when other locations in the Gairloch region are not suitable.

You will find plenty of boats moored in the cove and around the launch ramp. The piles of lobster pots all add to the atmosphere in this surprisingly busy little spot. The Badachro Inn has an incredible setting for a post Paddle refreshment.

The scenery is rather mind blowing with different vistas appearing at different points, from looking towards Gairloch to several small Islands including Eilean Horrisdale, which is joined on to the mainland at low tide.

Co-ordinates
57.734154,-5.764347

Nearest Place
Badachro has accommodation and food at the Badachro Inn while Gairloch has more facilities and options.

Off the Water
Explore the incredible mountains of the region on a Hike or Mountain Biking trip with www.climbrideexplore.co.uk

POOLEWE

Poolewe is famous for it's semi tropical climate and its historical gardens in which you can admire plants and palm trees not normally seen at this latitude. The village also makes a fantastic Paddleboarding destination as well. Situated in a sweeping semi circle on Loch Ewe, Poolewe offers a large amount of protection for the paddler while also encompassing stunning Highland views.

It should be noted that you should treat the area around the river mouth where Loch Maree joins Loch Ewe with some caution as there is a large amount of water moving in this area.

There are plenty of places to stay and eat, all adding to Poolewe being a most favourable location. A combination of paddling at Poolewe, Gairloch main beach and Badachro would be a fantastic introduction to North Coast 500 Paddleboarding, offering a mix of everything, Palm Trees, White Sands, Islands, Rock pools and mountain views.

Co-ordinates
57.767177,-5.601027

Nearest Place
Poolewe is a small village with places to eat and stay in it.

Off the Water
Inverewe Gardens is a lush, tropical collection of plants and trees from around the Globe. Since the Nineteenth century these gardens have used the unique Gulf Stream climate to create this beautiful space.

MATT GAMBLES

https://www.nts.org.uk/visit/places/inverewe

ACHMELVICH

Just a few miles down a single track road from the small fishing village of Lochinvar lies a little bit of Paddle Boarding Paradise. The road ends at the magical beach of Achmelvich. Picture white sands and an azure blue sea. It all can look decidedly tropical as long as you don't take the water and air temperature into account.

The water here can be that clear that, looking down from your board, what seems like a few feet below to the sandy bottom could be twenty or so feet. A surreal experience, especially at this high latitude.

From the main beach, in both directions there are several tiny hidden coves to explore and investigate. Achmelvich has a campsite (where you will park even if here for the day) so you can easily stay and explore the area further. With it facing west expect a stunning sunset as standard!.

Co-ordinates
58.169621,-5.302135

Nearest Place
There is a Campsite directly by the beach, for all other facilities head to the small Fishing port of Lochinvar, which you will pass to get to Achmelvich.

Off the Water
Eas Coul Aulin Waterfall. At 685ft, this is the longest Waterfall in the United Kingdom. To get there it's either a pretty long hike or a Summer Boat cruise to it.

MATT GAMBLES

http://kyleskuboattours.com/

DUNNET BEACH

The mile wide beach at Durness is home to some fantastic views across cliffs of Caithness and the clifftops running towards Thurso. With easy access from several small car parks and backed by dunes, Dunnet beach is a fantastic place to surf in the right conditions.
This part of the Caithness coast is famous for its powerful surf, including the World Class break of Thurso East. Most of these breaks are incredibly powerful and break into very shallow rock ledges, think breaking boards and super steep take offs. Dunnet offers you the opportunity to surf some North Shore power on a much more forgiving and Paddleboarding friendly beach break.

Co-ordinates
58.615671,-3.345621

Nearest Place
In the Summer, there is a small cafe and Campsite right by the beach car park. Nearby Castletown has a shop and garage, for more extensive facilities head to Thurso.

Off the Water
Just North of Dunnet Beach lies the 300 foot cliffs of Dunnet Head. These cliffs are the most Northerly point of mainland Britain and have incredible views of the Orkney Islands to the North.

MATT GAMBLES

STRATHY

Powerful waves ,golden sands and magnificent views are the order of the day at Strathy. This fine Surfing beach is situated on Scotland's North Coast, about 30 minutes drive West of Thurso. It is a fantastic place to score some heavy waves in a wonderful setting.

The beach has cliffs at either edge, the River Strathy pouring out at its Western edge and steep grassy banks in its centre. In the Summer they come magnificently to life and become covered with Wildflowers like Primrose and Kidney Vetch.

The view to the beach from the car park is worth visiting for alone. Situated next to a large, well kept Graveyard, looking down through the bright yellows, reds and green of the Flowers, past the towering cliffs and towards the distant Orkney Islands.

Co-ordinates
58.5636368, -3.9991498

Nearest Place
At the Car Park there is a Toilet and Shelter, which is a good place to get changed or maybe hide from inclement weather.
Strathy is a tiny, spread out village with a pub, the Strathy Inn. Melvich, a few miles east has a small shop and pub, with cabins to stay. For more choice then Thurso is further east again.

Off the Water
Take a hike to Strathy Point to admire the views from Strathy Lighthouse. Plenty of seabirds to spot on the cliffs and the view across the Pentland Firth towards the Orkney Islands is fantastic.

MATT GAMBLES

DURNESS

At the far North West of Scotland lies Durness. It is remote, it is wild and boy it is beautiful. It is a small but well spread out village and a great stopping point on the North Coast 500 driving route. Despite being remote it has several spots to stay, have a drink and some tiny shops to stock up on essentials.

It is blessed with Four beaches, all of which are stunning; Balnakiel, Sango Bay, Sango Beg and Ceannabeinne. Balnakiel faces west and is a white sand and azure blue waters stunner of a place when the weather plays ball. Backed by small sand dunes and with some small cliffs and tiny bays to explore at its northern side, on a calm day it is ripe for exploration, while when the surf comes through the bay it's a great place to experience the power of the Atlantic Ocean.

The other Three beaches all face North and are backed by some large, imposing Cliffs, offering a great juxtaposition with Balnakiel, just round the corner. They can produce some incredible surf.

Co-ordinates
Balnakiel - 58.576011,-4.767873
Sango Bay - 58.568097,-4.739774
Ceannabeinne - 58.547956,-4.676523

Nearest Place
Durness is a small but spread out settlement. It has a campsite, small shop, garage and a few places to stay and eat.

Off the Water

Between Sango Bay and Sango Beg lies Smoo Cave, a must visit. A large freshwater and Saltwater Cave leading right on to the beach, it can be explored on foot for free, or guided tour further in by boat.
www.smoocave.org

ABOUT THE AUTHOR

Matt Gambles

Owner of Paddle Surf Scotland, on of Scotland's oldest Stand Up Paddleboarding companies and partner in Breeze SUP Wear, Clothing Company.

Matt has contributed to several online Paddleboarding publications.

He has been Stand Up Paddleboarding for over 10 years and worked Worldwide in the Outdoor Adventure Industry for nearly 20 years.

Printed in Great Britain
by Amazon